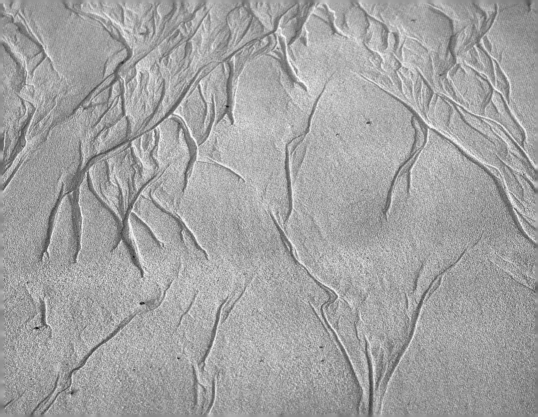

Published by Atmosphere
Willis Vean
Mullion Cornwall TR12 7DF
England
Tel 01326 240180

ISBN 978-0-9550805-1-7

Many of the pictures in this and other Atmosphere books are available as large
photo prints to frame. For details of sizes and prices see
www.atmosphere.co.uk/prints.html

To Jenny. Thanks for your patience.

ST IVES

Legend tells us that St Ives was founded by St Ia, an Irish saint who travelled to Cornwall in the 5th Century on a god-sent leaf. Realistically there was already a small settlement when she arrived. The town thrived and slowly developed as a port for shipping and fishing.

For many years fishing was the principle industry of the town and employed nearly all the inhabitants in one way or another.

Pigot's Directory described St Ives in 1823 in these words: *It has a very respectable and pleasing appearance, all the houses being handsomely covered with slated roofs, and in general well built; but on descending into the town, the streets are narrow, irregular, and ill paved. The church is an ancient gothic structure, built about 400 years ago. There are also chapels for the Methodists and Calvinists. The pilchard fishery is the principal support of the town; the season commences in July, and continues till the latter end of November; the mode of taking them is by the seine and drift nets. .... During the last season (1822) from the 10th of October to the 22d, about 3,400 hogsheads were taken, each hogshead containing 2,000 fish, all of which are cured and sent to the Italian markets.*

In 1844 The Directory wrote this: *The pilchard fishery is pursued here on a more extensive scale than upon any other part of the coast of Cornwall—in some years there are nearly two hundred seines employed. In prolific seasons, seventeen thousand hogsheads have been taken, each hogshead containing about two thousand fish, which are cured here, and chiefly sent to the Italian markets.*

In just 21 years the pilchard fishery had increased from 80 seines to 200. More was to come as Lake's Parochial History of 1868 describes: *Fish of almost every kind that frequent the coast are taken in St. Ives Bay; but the fishery absorbing all the others in its magnitude is the taking of pilchards. These are taken in two different ways quite distinct from each other.*

The first, the most ancient and most certain, and consequently of the greatest importance to the inhabitants of the locality, is called Drifting. In practising this method of fishing, the boats sail in the open sea, drawing after them very long nets, provided with small leads and corks at the opposite sides. The meshes of the nets are made of such size as to admit the head of a pilchard to pass through them, but not the body, the result is that such fish as strike against the net are retained suspended by the gills.

The second method is on a much more extensive scale, and somewhat uncertain as to success; but occasion-ally in prosperous seasons producing great wealth. This method is founded on the habit of pilchards to congregate in large shoals, and coming occasionally near the shore into shallow water, and into places where the ground is free from rocks; this latter circumstance is peculiarly favourable in S. Ives Bay, and the ground is moreover covered to the depth of several feet by a fine sand.

The seine or net used in this bay is between one hundred and fifty and two hundred fathoms long, and from seven to ten fathoms deep. More than two hundred and fifty of such nets are kept at S. Ives, every one having its own seine-boat to carry it. The nets are provided with heavy lead weights at one of their sides, so as to sink them firmly to the bottom, and with large corks to keep the other side to the surface of the water. Two large boats and one as an attendant, are appropriated to each net. When the huers stationed on the adjoining hills perceive a shoal of pilchards, they at once signal the boats and by signs give directions for their capture. The most common indication of a shoal of pilchards is a reddish line in the water, and the more compact the shoal the deeper is the hue.

As soon as the seine-boat and tow-boat are within reach of the shoal they start from the same point in opposite directions and are rowed rapidly around the fish, while the nets which they carry are being shot into the sea. When the seine and the stop-net meet they are immediately joined and form a circular wall round the fish about three hundred fathoms in circumference and reaching from the surface to the bottom. The Seine with its contents are then warped towards the shore into a secure part of the bay, and there moored with anchors so placed as to keep it as nearly circular as possible. Within the large net a small one called the tuck-net is introduced at low water for the purpose of raising the fish to the surface, when they are dipped up by baskets into the boats.

In 1834, an immense shoal passed into S. Ives Bay, and a portion remained in the waters on its western side, occupying the whole of the distance from the mouth of Hayle river to the town of S. Ives, more than two miles in a direct line, and in breadth about three-fourths of a mile. A seine was shot into this mass of fish and 120 boat loads, or 3600 hogsheads, were carried to the cellars,—each hogshead containing about 3000 pilchards.

In October 1846, a shoal of fish entered the bay and 30,000 hogsheads were enclosed, supposed to be about 75 millions of pilchards, the greatest quantity ever enclosed in one place at one time. Of these about 23,000 hogsheads were saved.

It seems lucky for St Ives that the Italians had a taste for pressed pilchards.

It is not only fishing which has provided St Ives with a fascinating history.

An atrocious incident happened during the Prayer Book Rebellion of 1549 when the Provost Marshall invited the mayor of St Ives, John Payne, to lunch at an Inn. During the meal a gallows was erected and the mayor was summarily hanged after the meal for being a Roman Catholic and by implication using the Latin prayer book.

The old service books had been abolished and the new English language Prayer Book ordered to be used. The Cornish people determined to resist these innovations. At that time the ancient Cornish language was the one spoken by the people, and it is probable that in St. Ives only a few could speak English; they clung to the old ways and to their ancient beliefs, and so entered heart and soul into the desperate venture of the Catholic Rebellion.

At the beginning of St Ives's prosperity in 1770 John Smeaton, the famous engineer, built the harbour wall known today as Smeaton's Pier with its distinctive octagonal lighthouse.

Just as the fishing industry was in decline the railway came to the town's rescue. St Ives became a holiday destination and a new round of business opportunity, with its ups and downs arrived. The Great

Ice cream

Western Railway Company operated Tregenna Castle at St Ives as a 'country house' hotel from 1878 a year after the line reached St Ives. This was one of the very first 'Resort Hotels' which were specifically aimed at patrons taking a week or more holiday.

With its sandy beaches now rapidly clearing of the pilchard fleet St Ives became the epitome of the English seaside destination.

Artists have found inspiration in St Ives and the surrounding area for nearly 200 years. J. M. W. Turner

visited in 1811 and again two years later. The 'plein air' movement in Pont-Aven, Brittany attracted several British artists who then looked for similar locations in England. They chose Newlyn and St Ives in Cornwall. James McNeil Whistler and Walter Sickert stayed in St Ives in 1883 working in the impressionistic style. Other artists from around the world came and established a presence which saw an

Artist's Club formed in 1888. Many artists visited for relatively short periods made possible by the arrival of the railway in 1877. Few lived full-time in the town until Bernard Leach arrived in 1920. Ben Nicholson and his wife Barbara Hepworth arrived in 1939 and became internationally famous. Other artists who came were John Wells, Wilhemina Barnes-Graham, Terry Frost and Bryan Wynter who were joined later by Patrick Heron, Roger Hilton and Sandra Blow. Together they and their contemporaries are associated with a distinctive English abstract style.

To honour the position the town holds in the art world the Tate St Ives Gallery was built and opened in 1993. Designed by Eldred Evans and David Shalev the gallery combines magnificent views of Porthmeor Beach from the interior and roof terrace.

RBARA HEPWORTH sculpture EPIDAUROUS donated by her to the people of St Ives.

THE HARBOUR at dawn enclosed by SMEATON'S PI

Boat mooring flo

Mooring rope and float.

Boat beached at low

Early morning harbour view. Steps on the harbour

Crab pots stacked on SMEATON'S PIER awaiting the crabbing seas

Self Drive pleasure boats await custome

dal pool reflection.

THE LIFEBOAT HOUSE and ST IA'S CHURCH from the harbour bea

A View of ST IVES from above the town.

Aerial view of the town with THE ISLAND IN THE FOREGROUN

ial view with the LIFEBOAT HOUSE in bottom left   Aerial view with SMEATON'S PIER in the foreground.   33

ST. IVES AT NIGHT

FORE STREET on a winter's afterno

SE LANE at night.

Wet cobbles on BUNKERS HILL in win

The TATE ST IVES

PORTHMEOR BEACH from the TATE ST IVES GALLERY.

THE TATE ST IVES at night.

PORTHGWIDDEN BEACH   THE ISLAND from the graveyard above PORTHMEOR BEA

Dawn at CARBIS BEACH.

Early morning in ST IVES B

PORTHMEOR BEACH

A seagull waits for snacks above PORTHMINSTER BEA

ES is surrounded by sandy beaches.

SS80